EMMANUEL JOSEPH

Sacred Synergy, Navigating Life with Faith, Morality, and Professional Success

Copyright © 2025 by Emmanuel Joseph

All rights reserved. No part of this publication may be reproduced, stored or transmitted in any form or by any means, electronic, mechanical, photocopying, recording, scanning, or otherwise without written permission from the publisher. It is illegal to copy this book, post it to a website, or distribute it by any other means without permission.

First edition

This book was professionally typeset on Reedsy.
Find out more at reedsy.com

Contents

1. Chapter 1 — 1
2. Chapter 1: The Intersection of Faith and Professional Life — 3
3. Chapter 2: Morality as the Foundation of Professional Ethics — 5
4. Chapter 3: Integrating Personal Values into Professional... — 7
5. Chapter 4: The Role of Compassion and Empathy in Leadership — 9
6. Chapter 5: The Power of Purpose-Driven Work — 11
7. Chapter 6: Ethical Entrepreneurship and Social... — 13
8. Chapter 7: The Synergy of Faith and Professional Ambition — 15
9. Chapter 8: Building a Legacy of Integrity and Impact — 17
10. Chapter 9: Navigating Ethical Dilemmas in the Workplace — 19
11. Chapter 10: The Importance of Work-Life Balance — 21
12. Chapter 11: The Power of Mindfulness and Spiritual Practices — 23
13. Chapter 12: Embracing a Holistic Approach to Life and Career — 25

1

Chapter 1

Introduction

In a world where the demands of professional success often seem to be at odds with the principles of faith and morality, finding a harmonious balance can feel like an insurmountable challenge. "Sacred Synergy: Navigating Life with Faith, Morality, and Professional Success" aims to address this very challenge by exploring the interconnectedness of these crucial aspects of life. This book seeks to provide readers with practical insights and strategies for achieving a fulfilling and balanced life, where professional ambitions and personal values can coexist harmoniously.

The journey toward professional success is often fraught with ethical dilemmas, challenges, and setbacks. However, by grounding oneself in faith and adhering to moral principles, individuals can navigate these obstacles with a clear conscience and a sense of purpose. This book delves into the ways in which faith can serve as a guiding light in the professional realm, providing the strength and resilience needed to persevere through difficulties and make ethical decisions.

At the heart of "Sacred Synergy" is the belief that personal values are not only compatible with professional success but can enhance and enrich one's career. By integrating personal values into professional life, individuals can experience greater job satisfaction, build meaningful relationships, and create a positive impact on their communities and organizations. This book offers practical tips and reflections to help readers identify their core values and align their careers with their beliefs.

Leadership plays a pivotal role in shaping organizational culture and fostering a positive work environment. Compassionate and empathetic leaders who act with integrity and fairness can inspire their teams to uphold high ethical standards and contribute to a supportive and inclusive workplace. "Sacred Synergy" explores the qualities of effective leadership and provides real-life examples of leaders who have successfully integrated faith and morality into their leadership styles.

In addition to exploring the personal and organizational dimensions of faith, morality, and professional success, this book also addresses the broader societal impact of ethical behavior and social responsibility. Ethical entrepreneurs and businesses that prioritize social and environmental impact can drive positive change and contribute to a more sustainable and equitable world. "Sacred Synergy" highlights the importance of ethical entrepreneurship and offers strategies for incorporating social responsibility into business practices.

Ultimately, "Sacred Synergy: Navigating Life with Faith, Morality, and Professional Success" is a guide for individuals seeking to live a holistic and fulfilling life. By embracing a holistic approach that considers the interconnectedness of all aspects of well-being, readers can achieve balance and harmony in both their personal and professional lives. This book invites readers to embark on a journey of self-discovery, reflection, and growth, where faith, morality, and professional success are not competing forces but complementary elements of a meaningful and impactful life.

2

Chapter 1: The Intersection of Faith and Professional Life

Faith has always played a significant role in the lives of many individuals, acting as a guiding light through various challenges and triumphs. In the realm of professional success, faith can often be the bedrock upon which individuals build their careers. This chapter delves into the ways in which faith can positively influence professional decisions, fostering a sense of purpose and direction. It explores personal stories of individuals who have seamlessly integrated their faith into their professional lives, leading to greater fulfillment and success.

One of the most profound aspects of faith is its ability to provide a moral compass, guiding individuals through ethical dilemmas and challenges in the workplace. By adhering to principles of integrity, honesty, and compassion, professionals can navigate complex situations with a clear conscience. This chapter highlights real-life scenarios where faith has played a crucial role in making difficult decisions, ultimately leading to positive outcomes.

Furthermore, faith can be a source of resilience and strength, helping individuals persevere through setbacks and failures. The professional journey is often fraught with obstacles, and it is during these times that faith can provide the necessary support to keep moving forward. Personal anecdotes and testimonies are shared to illustrate the transformative power of faith in overcoming adversity.

Another important aspect discussed in this chapter is the role of faith in building and maintaining relationships in the workplace. Strong, healthy relationships are essential for professional success, and faith can foster a sense of community and belonging. The chapter explores how faith-based values such as empathy, respect, and collaboration can enhance teamwork and create a positive work environment.

Lastly, this chapter addresses the importance of balancing faith and professional ambitions. It emphasizes that pursuing professional success does not have to come at the expense of one's faith. Instead, the two can coexist harmoniously, leading to a more holistic and fulfilling life. Practical tips and strategies are provided for maintaining this delicate balance.

3

Chapter 2: Morality as the Foundation of Professional Ethics

Morality is the cornerstone of ethical behavior in both personal and professional spheres. In this chapter, we explore the significance of morality in shaping professional ethics and conduct. It begins with an examination of the fundamental principles of morality and how they translate into ethical behavior in the workplace.

The chapter delves into the concept of moral leadership, where leaders exemplify ethical behavior and set the tone for the entire organization. By leading with integrity and fairness, leaders can inspire their teams to uphold high ethical standards. Real-life examples of moral leaders who have made a positive impact on their organizations are discussed, highlighting the far-reaching effects of ethical leadership.

Another key aspect of this chapter is the role of morality in decision-making. Ethical decision-making involves considering the well-being of all stakeholders and making choices that align with moral principles. The chapter presents various frameworks for ethical decision-making and provides practical examples of how these frameworks can be applied in professional settings.

The chapter also addresses the challenges and dilemmas that professionals may face when trying to uphold moral standards. It acknowledges that the workplace can be a complex environment where ethical boundaries are sometimes blurred. Through case studies and discussions, the chapter offers insights into navigating these challenges and making morally sound decisions.

Furthermore, the importance of creating an ethical organizational culture is emphasized. Organizations that prioritize ethical behavior and create a supportive environment for moral conduct are more likely to achieve long-term success. The chapter explores strategies for fostering an ethical culture, including the establishment of clear ethical guidelines, ongoing training, and open communication.

4

Chapter 3: Integrating Personal Values into Professional Life

Personal values are the deeply held beliefs that shape our behavior and decision-making. This chapter focuses on the integration of personal values into professional life, highlighting the benefits of aligning one's career with their core beliefs. It begins with an exploration of the concept of personal values and their influence on professional behavior.

The chapter discusses the process of identifying and articulating personal values. By gaining clarity on what truly matters to them, individuals can make more intentional career choices that align with their values. The chapter provides practical exercises and reflections to help readers identify their core values and understand how these values can guide their professional paths.

One of the key themes in this chapter is the importance of authenticity in the workplace. When individuals are true to their values, they are more likely to experience job satisfaction and a sense of fulfillment. The chapter presents real-life stories of professionals who have successfully integrated their personal values into their careers, leading to greater happiness and success.

The chapter also explores the potential conflicts that may arise when personal values clash with professional demands. It acknowledges that there may be situations where individuals must make difficult choices to uphold their values. Through case studies and discussions, the chapter offers strategies for navigating these conflicts and finding a balance between personal and professional integrity.

Additionally, the chapter emphasizes the role of personal values in shaping organizational culture. When individuals at all levels of an organization act in accordance with their values, it creates a positive and supportive work environment. The chapter explores ways in which organizations can encourage the expression of personal values and foster a culture of authenticity and integrity.

5

Chapter 4: The Role of Compassion and Empathy in Leadership

Compassion and empathy are essential qualities for effective leadership. This chapter delves into the importance of these qualities in fostering a positive and inclusive work environment. It begins with an exploration of the concepts of compassion and empathy and their relevance to leadership.

The chapter discusses the impact of compassionate leadership on employee well-being and engagement. Leaders who demonstrate empathy and understanding can build strong, trusting relationships with their teams, leading to higher levels of morale and productivity. Real-life examples of compassionate leaders who have made a positive impact on their organizations are presented to illustrate the benefits of this leadership style.

One of the key themes in this chapter is the role of empathy in decision-making. Empathetic leaders consider the perspectives and feelings of their employees when making decisions, leading to more inclusive and thoughtful outcomes. The chapter presents various strategies for developing and demonstrating empathy in leadership, including active listening, open communication, and emotional intelligence.

The chapter also addresses the challenges and potential pitfalls of compassionate leadership. It acknowledges that while compassion and empathy are important, leaders must also balance these qualities with the need for accountability and performance. Through case studies and discussions, the chapter offers insights into finding this balance and effectively leading with compassion.

Furthermore, the chapter explores the role of compassion and empathy in conflict resolution. Conflicts are inevitable in any organization, and empathetic leaders are better equipped to navigate these situations and find constructive solutions. The chapter provides practical tips and strategies for resolving conflicts with empathy and understanding.

6

Chapter 5: The Power of Purpose-Driven Work

Purpose-driven work is the idea that individuals are more motivated and fulfilled when their work aligns with a greater sense of purpose. This chapter explores the significance of purpose in the professional sphere and how it can lead to greater job satisfaction and success. It begins with an examination of the concept of purpose and its relevance to work.

The chapter discusses the benefits of having a clear sense of purpose in one's career. When individuals understand the larger impact of their work, they are more likely to feel motivated and engaged. The chapter presents real-life examples of professionals who have found purpose in their work and the positive effects it has had on their careers.

One of the key themes in this chapter is the process of discovering and defining one's purpose. The chapter provides practical exercises and reflections to help readers identify their passions and understand how they can contribute to a greater good through their work. It emphasizes that purpose is a deeply personal and evolving concept, and individuals may need to revisit and refine their sense of purpose over time.

The chapter also explores the role of organizations in supporting purpose-driven work. Organizations that prioritize purpose and create opportunities for employees to connect with their work on a deeper level are more likely to achieve long-term success. The chapter discusses various strategies for fostering a purpose-driven culture, including aligning organizational goals with social impact, offering opportunities for meaningful work, and recognizing and celebrating employees' contributions.

Additionally, the chapter addresses potential challenges and obstacles in pursuing purpose-driven work. It acknowledges that finding and maintaining a sense of purpose in one's career can be challenging, especially in the face of external pressures and demands. Through case studies and discussions, the chapter offers insights and strategies for overcoming these challenges and staying connected to one's purpose.

7

Chapter 6: Ethical Entrepreneurship and Social Responsibility

Entrepreneurship is often seen as a path to financial success and innovation. However, ethical entrepreneurship goes beyond profit-making and focuses on creating positive social impact. This chapter explores the principles of ethical entrepreneurship and the role of social responsibility in business.

The chapter begins with an examination of the concept of ethical entrepreneurship and its importance in today's business landscape. It discusses the idea that businesses have a responsibility to contribute to the well-being of society and the environment. The chapter presents real-life examples of ethical entrepreneurs who have built successful businesses while prioritizing social and environmental impact.

One of the key themes in this chapter is the integration of social responsibility into business practices. Ethical entrepreneurs consider the impact of their decisions on all stakeholders, including employees, customers, suppliers, and the community. The chapter explores various strategies for incorporating social responsibility into business operations, such as sustainable sourcing, fair labor practices, and community engagement.

The chapter also addresses the challenges and dilemmas that ethical entrepreneurs may face. It acknowledges that balancing profit-making with social responsibility can be complex and challenging. Through case studies and discussions, the chapter offers insights into navigating these challenges and making ethical decisions that align with one's values.

Furthermore, the chapter explores the role of ethical entrepreneurship in driving positive change. Ethical entrepreneurs have the potential to create innovative solutions to social and environmental issues, leading to a more sustainable and equitable world. The chapter discusses various examples of businesses that have successfully integrated social responsibility into their models and the positive impact they have achieved.

Additionally, the chapter emphasizes the importance of fostering a culture of ethics and social responsibility within organizations. Ethical entrepreneurs lead by example and create environments where employees are encouraged to act with integrity and contribute to positive social impact. The chapter provides practical tips and provides strategies for creating an ethical organizational culture, including clear ethical guidelines, ongoing training, and open communication.

8

Chapter 7: The Synergy of Faith and Professional Ambition

In this chapter, we explore the harmonious relationship between faith and professional ambition. Many individuals struggle with the notion that pursuing professional success may come at the expense of their faith. However, this chapter emphasizes that faith and ambition can coexist and even complement each other, leading to a more fulfilling life.

The chapter begins by discussing the concept of vocation, which is the idea that one's professional work can be a calling or mission. By viewing their careers as a vocation, individuals can find deeper meaning and purpose in their work, aligning their professional ambitions with their faith. Real-life examples of individuals who have found their vocations are presented to illustrate this concept.

One of the key themes in this chapter is the importance of setting goals that align with one's faith and values. The chapter provides practical tips and reflections for setting meaningful and achievable goals that honor both professional ambitions and spiritual beliefs. It emphasizes that success is not solely defined by external achievements but also by internal fulfillment and alignment with one's values.

The chapter also explores the role of faith in overcoming challenges and setbacks in the pursuit of professional ambitions. Faith can provide the strength and resilience needed to persevere through difficulties and maintain a positive outlook. Personal stories of individuals who have relied on their faith during challenging times are shared to highlight the transformative power of faith.

Furthermore, the chapter addresses the potential conflicts that may arise when professional ambitions clash with faith-based values. It acknowledges that there may be situations where individuals must make difficult choices to uphold their faith. Through case studies and discussions, the chapter offers strategies for navigating these conflicts and finding a balance between professional success and spiritual integrity.

9

Chapter 8: Building a Legacy of Integrity and Impact

Building a legacy of integrity and impact is a goal that many individuals aspire to achieve. This chapter explores the importance of leaving a positive and lasting legacy in both personal and professional spheres. It begins with an examination of the concept of legacy and its significance in shaping one's life and career.

The chapter discusses the role of integrity in building a legacy. Acting with honesty, fairness, and ethical behavior creates a strong foundation for a positive legacy. The chapter presents real-life examples of individuals who have built legacies of integrity and the positive impact they have had on their communities and organizations.

One of the key themes in this chapter is the importance of making a positive impact through one's work. The chapter explores various ways in which individuals can contribute to the well-being of others and society as a whole. It emphasizes that making a difference is not limited to grand gestures but can be achieved through everyday actions and decisions.

The chapter also addresses the challenges and obstacles that may arise in the pursuit of building a legacy. It acknowledges that maintaining integrity and making a positive impact can be challenging in the face of external pressures and demands. Through case studies and discussions, the chapter offers insights and strategies for overcoming these challenges and staying true to one's values.

Furthermore, the chapter emphasizes the role of mentorship and leadership in building a legacy. By guiding and inspiring others, individuals can extend their positive impact and create a ripple effect that lasts beyond their lifetimes. The chapter provides practical tips and reflections for becoming a mentor and leader who leaves a lasting legacy of integrity and impact.

10

Chapter 9: Navigating Ethical Dilemmas in the Workplace

Ethical dilemmas are an inevitable part of professional life, and navigating them requires a strong moral compass and ethical decision-making skills. This chapter explores common ethical dilemmas that professionals may encounter in the workplace and provides strategies for addressing them.

The chapter begins with an examination of the nature of ethical dilemmas and the factors that contribute to their complexity. It discusses the importance of understanding the broader context and considering the perspectives of all stakeholders when faced with an ethical dilemma.

One of the key themes in this chapter is the role of ethical frameworks in decision-making. The chapter presents various ethical frameworks, such as utilitarianism, deontology, and virtue ethics, and explains how they can be applied to resolve ethical dilemmas. Practical examples and case studies are provided to illustrate the application of these frameworks in professional settings.

The chapter also addresses the importance of seeking guidance and support when navigating ethical dilemmas. It emphasizes that professionals do not have to face these challenges alone and can seek advice from mentors, colleagues, and ethics committees. The chapter provides practical tips for identifying and approaching trusted sources of support.

Furthermore, the chapter explores the role of organizational culture in shaping ethical behavior. Organizations that prioritize ethics and create a supportive environment for ethical decision-making are more likely to achieve positive outcomes. The chapter discusses various strategies for fostering an ethical organizational culture, including clear ethical guidelines, ongoing training, and open communication.

Lastly, the chapter addresses the potential consequences of ethical decision-making, both positive and negative. It acknowledges that making ethical choices may sometimes come at a cost, such as personal or professional repercussions. Through case studies and discussions, the chapter offers insights into navigating these consequences and staying true to one's values.

11

Chapter 10: The Importance of Work-Life Balance

Work-life balance is a crucial aspect of maintaining overall well-being and achieving long-term success. This chapter explores the significance of work-life balance and provides practical strategies for achieving it. It begins with an examination of the concept of work-life balance and its relevance in today's fast-paced world.

The chapter discusses the benefits of achieving work-life balance, including improved physical and mental health, increased job satisfaction, and better relationships. Real-life examples of individuals who have successfully achieved work-life balance are presented to illustrate these benefits.

One of the key themes in this chapter is the importance of setting boundaries and prioritizing self-care. The chapter provides practical tips and reflections for setting boundaries between work and personal life and ensuring that self-care is a priority. It emphasizes that taking care of oneself is essential for maintaining overall well-being and achieving long-term success.

The chapter also addresses the challenges and obstacles that may arise in the pursuit of work-life balance. It acknowledges that finding balance can be challenging, especially in demanding and high-pressure environments. Through case studies and discussions, the chapter offers insights and strategies for overcoming these challenges and achieving work-life balance.

Furthermore, the chapter explores the role of organizations in supporting work-life balance. Organizations that prioritize work-life balance and create a supportive environment for employees are more likely to achieve positive outcomes. The chapter discusses various strategies for fostering a work-life balance culture, including flexible work arrangements, wellness programs, and open communication.

Lastly, the chapter emphasizes the importance of continuous self-reflection and adjustment in achieving work-life balance. It acknowledges that work-life balance is not a static state but an ongoing process that requires continuous effort and adjustment. The chapter provides practical tips and reflections for maintaining work-life balance over time.

12

Chapter 11: The Power of Mindfulness and Spiritual Practices

Mindfulness and spiritual practices can be powerful tools for enhancing overall well-being and achieving professional success. This chapter explores the benefits of mindfulness and spiritual practices and provides practical strategies for incorporating them into daily life.

The chapter begins with an examination of the concept of mindfulness and its relevance to professional life. It discusses the benefits of mindfulness, including increased focus, reduced stress, and improved emotional regulation. Real-life examples of individuals who have successfully incorporated mindfulness into their professional lives are presented to illustrate these benefits.

One of the key themes in this chapter is the importance of cultivating a regular mindfulness practice. The chapter provides practical tips and reflections for developing a mindfulness practice, including meditation, breathing exercises, and mindful movement. It emphasizes that mindfulness is a skill that can be developed with regular practice and effort.

The chapter also explores the role of spiritual practices in enhancing overall well-being and achieving professional success. It discusses various spiritual practices, such as prayer, journaling, and gratitude, and their potential benefits. Practical tips and reflections are provided for incorporating these practices into daily life.

Furthermore, the chapter addresses the challenges and obstacles that may arise in the pursuit of mindfulness and spiritual practices. It acknowledges that finding time and maintaining consistency can be challenging, especially in busy and demanding environments. Through case studies and discussions, the chapter offers insights and strategies for overcoming these challenges and maintaining a regular practice.

Lastly, the chapter emphasizes the importance of integrating mindfulness and spiritual practices into the workplace. Organizations that prioritize mindfulness and create opportunities for employees to engage in spiritual practices are more likely to achieve positive outcomes. The chapter discusses various strategies for fostering a mindfulness culture, including mindfulness training, quiet spaces, and supportive leadership.

13

Chapter 12: Embracing a Holistic Approach to Life and Career

In the final chapter, we explore the importance of embracing a holistic approach to life and career. A holistic approach considers the interconnectedness of all aspects of life, including physical, mental, emotional, and spiritual well-being. This chapter emphasizes that true success and fulfillment come from achieving balance and harmony in all areas of life.

The chapter begins with an examination of the concept of holistic well-being and its relevance to professional life. It discusses the benefits of a holistic approach, including improved overall well-being, increased job satisfaction, and better relationships. Real-life examples of individuals who have successfully embraced a holistic approach are presented to illustrate these benefits.

One of the key themes in this chapter is the importance of self-awareness and self-reflection in achieving holistic well-being. The chapter provides practical tips and reflections for developing self-awareness and understanding one's needs and priorities. It emphasizes that self-awareness is essential for making intentional choices that align with one's values and goals.

The chapter also explores the role of balance and harmony in achieving holistic well-being. It discusses various strategies for achieving balance and harmony in all areas of life, including work, relationships, self-care, and spiritual practices. Practical tips and reflections are provided for integrating these strategies into daily life.

Furthermore, the chapter addresses the challenges and obstacles that may arise in the pursuit of holistic well-being. It acknowledges that achieving balance and harmony can be challenging, especially in busy and demanding environments. Through case studies and discussions, the chapter offers insights and strategies for overcoming these challenges and achieving achieving holistic well-being.

The chapter emphasizes the importance of continuous self-reflection and adjustment in achieving a holistic approach to life and career. It acknowledges that holistic well-being is an ongoing process that requires effort and intentionality. The chapter provides practical tips and reflections for maintaining balance and harmony over time.

Additionally, the chapter explores the role of organizations in supporting holistic well-being. Organizations that prioritize the well-being of their employees and create supportive environments are more likely to achieve positive outcomes. The chapter discusses various strategies for fostering a holistic culture, including wellness programs, flexible work arrangements, and supportive leadership.

In conclusion, this chapter encourages readers to embrace a holistic approach to life and career, recognizing the interconnectedness of all aspects of well-being. It emphasizes that true success and fulfillment come from achieving balance and harmony in all areas of life. Practical tips and reflections are provided to guide readers on their journey toward holistic well-being.

Book Description: Sacred Synergy: Navigating Life with Faith, Morality, and Professional Success

"**Sacred Synergy: Navigating Life with Faith, Morality, and Professional Success**" is an enlightening guide for individuals seeking to harmonize their professional ambitions with their faith and moral values. This compelling book explores the intricate balance between career advancement and personal integrity, offering practical insights and strategies for achieving a

CHAPTER 12: EMBRACING A HOLISTIC APPROACH TO LIFE AND CAREER

fulfilling and balanced life.

The book delves into the profound ways faith can influence professional decisions, providing a moral compass that guides individuals through ethical dilemmas and challenges in the workplace. It highlights real-life stories of professionals who have seamlessly integrated their faith into their careers, leading to greater fulfillment and success.

Readers will discover the significance of personal values in shaping professional behavior and the importance of authenticity in the workplace. Through practical exercises and reflections, the book helps readers identify their core values and align their careers with their beliefs, resulting in a more meaningful and satisfying professional journey.

Leadership is a central theme in "Sacred Synergy," with a focus on compassionate and empathetic leadership that fosters a positive and inclusive work environment. The book presents inspiring examples of leaders who have exemplified integrity and fairness, creating a supportive culture that encourages ethical behavior and teamwork.

In addition to personal and organizational dimensions, the book addresses the broader societal impact of ethical behavior and social responsibility. It emphasizes the role of ethical entrepreneurship in driving positive change and offers strategies for incorporating social responsibility into business practices.

Ultimately, "Sacred Synergy: Navigating Life with Faith, Morality, and Professional Success" is a comprehensive guide for individuals seeking to live a holistic and fulfilling life. By embracing a holistic approach that considers the interconnectedness of all aspects of well-being, readers can achieve balance and harmony in both their personal and professional lives. This book invites readers to embark on a journey of self-discovery, reflection, and growth, where faith, morality, and professional success are not competing forces but complementary elements of a meaningful and impactful life.

www.ingramcontent.com/pod-product-compliance
Lightning Source LLC
LaVergne TN
LVHW020742090526
838202LV00057BA/6187